GCSE

Mathematics
Intermediate Level

Sheila Hunt and
Philip Hooper

Hodder & Stoughton

A MEMBER OF THE HODDER HEADLINE GROUP

Using Mind Maps® in your revision

Mind Maps® can be a valuable aid to revision. They help you organise your thoughts in a logical and easy-to-remember format. Sample Mind Maps® are provided on pages 30 and 88. Look at these. Try to use the model to help you revise other topics.

The "Teach Yourself" name and logo are registered trade marks of Hodder & Stoughton Ltd in the UK.

A catalogue record for this title is available from the British Library.

ISBN 0 340 74705 X

First published 1999
Impression number   10 9 8 7 6 5 4 3 2 1
Year   2000 1999

Editorial, design and production by Hart McLeod, Cambridge

Printed in Great Britain for Hodder & Stoughton Educational, a division of Hodder Headline Plc, 338 Euston Road, London NW1 3BH

Rapid Revision Planner

Shape and Space Step 1

Handling Data Step 1

Numbers Step 2

Algebra Step 2

For a start

A reminder:

- $<$ means less than
- $\leqslant$ less than or equals
- $>$ greater than
- $\geqslant$ greater than or equals
- $\sqrt{}$ square root
- $\sqrt[3]{}$ cube root
- $\approx$ roughly equal to

$x < 3$ x is any value up to 3 excluding 3 itself
$y \leqslant 3$ y is any value up to and including 3
$x > 3$ x is greater than 3
$y \geqslant 3$ $y = 3$ or any value greater than 3
$\sqrt{25} = 5$ (or -5) $5^2 = 25$
$\sqrt[3]{8} = 2$ $2^3 = 8$
1 kg ≈ 2.2 pounds

Using a calculator

A **scientific** calculator works like this:

- 1st   **Brackets**
- 2nd   **Of** as in 3 to the power of 4
  – i.e. 3^4
- 3rd   **Divide**
- 4th   **Multiply**
- 5th   **Add**
- 6th   **Subtract.**

Your teacher may use BIDMAS where I = Indices. Check you can use your calculator to:

- square and square root
- do fractions
- work out standard form
- solve Pythagoras and trigonometry questions.

$(\ )$ x^y $\div$ $\times$ $+$ $-$

7

Number basics

Numbers

Just to recap.
If there is no sign in front of a number,
imagine +. For example, $6 = {}^+6$
$3 + 5 = 8$; $-3 + 5 = 2$
$3 - 5 = -2$; $-3 - 5 = -8$

Directed numbers

Two signs side by side – if the signs are the:

- **same**, replace with **plus** (both 4 letters)
- for example
$2 + {}^+5 = 2 + 5 = 7$; $2 - {}^-5 = 2 + 5 = 7$
- **dIfferent**, replace with **mInus** (both have letter "**I**")
- for example,
$2 + {}^-5 = 2 - 5 = -3$; $2 - {}^+5 = 2 - 5 = -3$.

Multiplying and dividing directed numbers

- same sign $\rightarrow \boxed{+}$; for example,
$4 \times 3 = 12$; $-4 \times -3 = 12$
- different signs $\rightarrow \boxed{-}$; for example,
$4 \times -3 = -12$; $-4 \times 3 = -12$.

The same rules apply for division.

Now move on to **TRIPLETS** – these simple techniques hold the key to many common examination questions.

Triplets

This technique can help with many questions.

In algebra, this triplet represents
$a = b \times c$
$b = a \div c$ or $b = \frac{a}{c}$
$c = a \div b$ or $\frac{a}{b}$

Example

(**D**owning **S**tree**T**)

Distance = **S**peed × **T**ime

$$\text{**S**peed} = \frac{\text{**D**istance}}{\text{**T**ime}} \qquad \text{**T**ime} = \frac{\text{**D**istance}}{\text{**S**peed}}$$

Triplets in action

- Write down the triplet.
- Cover or cross out the letter which represents the quantity which you wish to find.
- If the remaining letters are on the same level multiply them together; if not, divide the top by the bottom.

For example, a car travels at 70 km/h. How long does it take to go 157.5 km?

$T = \dfrac{D}{S} = \dfrac{157.5}{70} = 2.25$ hr = 2 hr 15 min.

Note: 0.25 hr = 0.25 × 60 min = 15 min.

Triplets – continued

The ART of filling containers

Art – **A**mount, **R**ate, **T**ime.

The density formula for the Very Dense

Mass, **V**olume, **D**ensity – use mass for questions involving weight.

Most things are **V**ery **D**ifficult if you are **V**ery **D**ense.

Circumference of a circle

Circumference = $\pi \times$ **D**.
Diameter = $\dfrac{\text{Circumference}}{\pi}$.

Imagine π as a table with a terrified cat on top and a furious dog underneath!
(You may also see $C = 2\pi r$.)

Trigonometry

See also • **Trigonometry** pp. 37–42

Direct proportionality – X-Direct method

Use X-Direct in all sorts of ways. Here is a simple example.

If four books cost £20, find the cost of six books.

Conventional method		Short cut, using X-direct	
books	cost in £	books	cost in £
4	20	4 ⟍	20 **T**imes the **T**wo
1	$\frac{20}{4} = 5$	✕	**slide** and **divide** by the other.
6	$5 \times 6 = £30$	6	$\frac{6 \times 20}{4} = £30$

Some uses of X-Direct – Comparing quantities

For example, 3.2 litres of liquid contain 850 grams of a chemical. (**a**) How many grams are in 7.5 litres? (**b**) How many litres contain 1.4 kilograms of the chemical?

(a)	litres	grams	(b)	litres	grams
I know	3.2	800		3.2	800
I need	7.5	$\frac{7.5 \times 800}{3.2}$		$\frac{3.2 \times 1400}{800}$	1400
		= 1875 grams		= 5.6 litres	

Changing money

For example, when the rate was 3.4 German marks (DM) to £1.00 (**a**) how many pounds were worth 150 DM? and (**b**) how many DM were worth £145.20?

(a)	DM	£	(b)	DM	£
I know	3.4	1		3.4	1
I need	150	$\frac{150 \times 1}{3.4}$		$\frac{3.4 \times 145.20}{1}$	145.20
		= £44.12		= 493.68 DM	

(Leaving out × 1 or ÷ 1 won't affect the answer.)

Pie charts and percentages

Pie charts

For example, the results of a survey of 540
people were represented on a pie chart.
(**a**) How many degrees would represent
24 people? (**b**) How many people would be
represented by 158°? Use X-Direct.

(**a**)	degrees	people	(**b**)	degrees	people
I know	360	540		360	540
I need	$\frac{360 \times 24}{540}$	24		158	$\frac{158 \times 540}{360}$
	= 16°				= 237 people

Percentages

Remember: the whole amount is 100%.
For example, (**a**) find 35% of £870 and
(**b**) what percentage is 67 out of 175?
Use X-Direct.

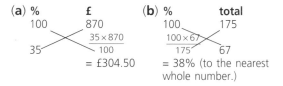

(**a**) %   £
    100   870
                $\frac{35 \times 870}{100}$
    35
             = £304.50

(**b**) %   total
    100   175
             $\frac{100 \times 67}{175}$
    175   67
             = 38% (to the nearest
             whole number.)

Note:

You can put the columns either way round,
times the **t**wo on the top, **slide** and **divide**
by the other underneath.

Ratios

Divide 75 in the ratio 3:2.
(3:2 = 3 to 2, 5 parts altogether.)

$75 \div 5 = 15$
$3 \times 15 = 45$
$2 \times 15 = 30$
Answer: 45:30.

Brown paint is made using 3 parts red to 2 parts green to 1 part yellow. How many litres of each are needed to make 24 litres of brown paint? (Six parts altogether)

$24 \div 6 = 4$
$3 \times 4 = 12$
$2 \times 4 = 8, 1 \times 4 = 4$

Answer: 12 l red, 8 l green, 4 l yellow.

Two people shared some money in the ratio 4:3. If the larger share was £32, what was the smaller?

shares   £
4   32
          $\dfrac{3 \times 32}{4}$
3
          = £24

Express the ratio 15:75 in its simplest form.
Cancel to lowest terms (divide both by 3 and 5, or by 15 in one step). **Answer** 1:5.

Express the ratio $1.4 \times 10^8 : 3.2 \times 10^{12}$ in the form (a) n:1 and (b) 1:n.

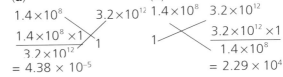

(a)
$1.4 \times 10^8 \qquad 3.2 \times 10^{12}$
$\dfrac{1.4 \times 10^8 \times 1}{3.2 \times 10^{12}} \quad 1$
$= 4.38 \times 10^{-5}$

(b)
$1.4 \times 10^8 \qquad 3.2 \times 10^{12}$
$1 \quad \dfrac{3.2 \times 10^{12} \times 1}{1.4 \times 10^8}$
$= 2.29 \times 10^4$

Direct and inverse proportion

Direct proportion

Use the ratio ruler or X-Direct.
To spot X-Direct questions, look for:

- ...is proportional to...
- ...is directly proportional to...
- ...varies directly with...

Inverse proportion

Questions usually say:

- ...is inversely proportional to...
- ...is indirectly proportional to...
- ...varies inversely with...

(**a**) For example, a car, being driven at 80 km/h takes 6 hours to complete a journey. How long would it take at 40 km/h?

Answer – Half the speed, therefore twice the time: 12 hours.

(**b**) Six men build a wall in three days. How long would it take nine men?

men	days	
6	3	
1	6 × 3 = 18	**M**ultiply **A**nd
9	18 ÷ 9 = 2	then **D**ivide

Inverse proportion can drive you MAD!
Use **MAD** in questions which say:

- ...inversely proportional to...
- ...varies indirectly with...
- ...varies inversely with...

Percentages

There are many ways of achieving the correct result. Try these ideas for yourself.

Basic percentages – % increase/decrease

(**a**) A coat costing £90 is reduced by 15%. Find the new price.

£	%	or	£	%
90	100		90	100

$\frac{90 \times 15}{100}$ 15 $\frac{90 \times 85}{100}$ 85

gives £13.50   (100% − 15% = 85%)
(not £13.5),
then £90 − £13.50   = £76.50 (not £76.5).

(**b**) The weight of a 450 g tin was increased by 12%. Find its new weight.

%	g	or	%	g
100	450		100	450

12   $\frac{450 \times 12}{100}$ 112 $\frac{450 \times 112}{100}$

                      (100 + 12 = 112)

gives 54 g then
450 g + 54 g   = 504 g.

Finding 100%

In a school, 20% of pupils had 'flu. A total of 160 children were ill; how many pupils did the school have?

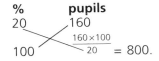

%	pupils
20	160
100	$\frac{160 \times 100}{20}$ = 800.

15

Percentages – continued

Percentages and decimals

$10\% = \frac{10}{100} = 0.1$ $50\% = \frac{50}{100} = 0.5$ etc.
$17.5\% = 0.175$ (for VAT questions).

For example: Remember: **of** = ×
Find 35% **of** £120.00.   **out of** = ÷
$35\% = 0.35 \times £120.00 = £42.00$.

In a test, a pupil scored 27 **out of** 75. What
percentage was that?

27 out of $75 = \frac{27}{75} = 27 \div 75 = 0.36$.

$0.36 = \frac{36}{100} = 36\%$ (or $0.36 \times 100 = 36\%$).

DAFT about % increase/decrease

For example: a car bought for £8500.00 is sold
for £6000.00. Find the percentage
decrease/percentage loss to nearest 1%.

Actual loss = £2500.00

For % profit/loss always put the:

Difference **A**bove the **F**irs**T** number, (and you
are **DAFT** if you forget!)
i.e. $\frac{2500}{8500} = 0.294 = 29\%$.

Decimal places and significant figures

Decimal places

- Decimal places = no. of digits after decimal point.
- Ring digit one place to right of required digit.
- Number ringed is ≥ 5 ↑ round up, number ringed is <5 ↓ round down.
- Examples: 4.7385 = 4.739 (3 d.p.); 4.7385 = 4.74 (2 d.p.); 4.7385 = 4.7 (1 d.p.).
- Use a zero to make up required d.p.
- Examples: 4.697 = 4.70 (2 d.p.); 6.98 = 7.0 (1 d.p. or to nearest 0.1).

Significant figures

- Count from first non zero digit from left.
- Don't count zeros at end, for example 134 000 = 3 s.f.; 0.00002 = 1 s.f.
- Round as for decimal places, for example 5.268 = 5.3 (2 s.f.); 0.0039 = 0.004 (1 s.f.).
- 3871= 4000 (1 s.f.) 3900 (2 s.f.) 3870 (3 s.f.). Be careful to put enough noughts. Don't write 4, 39 or 387!

Note: Be careful when rounding – if you need 3.2 bottles of squash you must round up to 4 bottles to avoid thirsty customers!

Smallest and largest values

(a) The number 350 is given to the nearest 50. What are the smallest and largest values?

Line drawn to show mid-point.

Answer: smallest = 325, largest = 375.

(b) The number 3.2 is given to the nearest 0.1. What are the smallest and largest values?

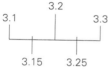

Answer: smallest = 3.15, largest = 3.25.

Standard/Standard index form

Standard form

Standard form is used to write very large or small numbers as powers of ten.
For example, (**a**) write 342 000 000 000 in standard form.

• Insert a decimal point after the first non-zero digit starting from the left: 3.42.
• "Jump" the point back to its starting position – 3.42 000 000 000.
• Write this as a power of 10 – 3.42×10^{11}.

(**b**) Write 368957.12 in standard form to 3 significant figures: 3.68957.12
$= 3.69 \times 10^5$.

For numbers <1
(**c**) Write 0.00000047 in standard form –
$0.0000004.7 = 4.7 \times 10^{-7}$.

Calculator

Most calculators have $\boxed{\text{EE}}$ or $\boxed{\text{EXP}}$.

• **Replace** "times ten to the" by $\boxed{\text{EXP}}$ or $\boxed{\text{EE}}$.
• Value 3.42 **times** ten to the eleven
$\overset{\text{PRESS}}{\rightarrow}$ 3.42 $\boxed{\text{EXP}}$/$\boxed{\text{EE}}$ 11.

• **Do not key 3.42 $\times$ 10** $\boxed{\text{EXP}}$ **11**: the answer will be 10 times too big!
• Value 4.7 **times** ten to the **minus** seven
$\overset{\text{PRESS}}{\rightarrow}$ 4.7 $\boxed{\text{EXP}}$/$\boxed{\text{EE}}$ –7 (**not** 4.7 $\times$ 10 $\boxed{\text{EE}}$ –7).

Remember **standard form** and **standard index form** mean the same.

Powers / Indices

Powers = indices
$3^4 = 3 \times 3 \times 3 \times 3 = 3$ to the power of 4.
$3^4 = 81.$

TIPS on using indices

Ensure basic numbers (bottom numbers) are the same, then:

- **TIP** (**T**imes = **I**ndices **P**lus) $2^3 \times 2^5 = 2^8$
- **DIM** (**D**ivide = **I**ndices **M**inus) $5^5 \div 5^2 = 5^3$.

Also:

- x^0 (i.e. any number to the power of zero) $= 1$, for example, $2^0 = 5^0 = 21^0 = 135^0 = 1$
- $x^{1/2}$ $\sqrt{x}$ (square root)
- $x^{1/3} = \sqrt[3]{x}$ (cube root)
- $x^{-1} = \frac{1}{x}$.

Calculator

Use either $\boxed{y^x}$ or $\boxed{x^y}$ depending on calculator.

2^8 means 2 to the power of 8 or
$2 \times 2 \times 2 \times 2 \times 2 \times 2 \times 2 \times 2$.
$2^8 = 2 \boxed{y^x} 8 = 256.$ or $2 \boxed{x^y} 8 = 256.$

Note: Don't **confuse** $\boxed{y^x}$ or $\boxed{x^y}$ with $\boxed{EE}$ or $\boxed{EXP}$.

You can use $\boxed{EE}$ or $\boxed{EXP}$ when you can say "times 10 to the ...".

2×10^8 means
2×10 to the 8
$= 2 \boxed{EXP} 8$
$= 200\ 000\ 000.$

Algebra basics

- $2a = a + a$ or $2 \times a$
- $a^2 = a \times a$
- $3a^2 = 3 \times a \times a$
- $(3a)^2 = 3a \times 3a = 9a^2$.

Expressions, equations and inequalities:

- $5t + 3z$ is an expression
- $5y = 20$ is an equation
- $2x < 10$ is an inequality.

Terms: (items)

- $3y - 2z$ has 2 terms
- $6a^2 + a - 4$ has 3 terms.

Vocabulary

For example, $3x^2 - 7x + 2.5$

- **Variable:** letter representing a number (x^2, x).
- **Coefficient:** number with a variable ($\mathbf{3}x^2$, $\mathbf{-7}x$).
- **Constant:** number without a variable (2.5).

Calculations

Remember directed numbers, for example:
$6y + 2y = 8y$, $6y - 2y = 4y$, $2y - 5y = -3y$,
$4g \times 2 = 8g$, $-3 \times 2b = -6b$,
$3f \times 4f = 12f^2$, $-2d \times 5d = -10d^2$,
$-4e \times -2e = 8e^2$, $16c \div 2c = 8$,
$12m^2 \div 3m = 4m$.

Equation basics

Variable – letter (x, y etc.).
Coefficient – number with letter ($4x$, $13y^2$).
Constant – number without letter (2, 19).

To solve an equation:

• get variables on one side, constants on the other
• do same operations (+, −, ×, ÷) to both sides of equation.

or
(**a**)$x + 3 = 10$ −3 both sides $x + 3 = 10$
$x\quad = 10 - 3$ $\quad\quad\underline{-3\quad -3}$
$x\quad = 7$ $x\quad = 7$

or
(**b**)$x - 2 = 12$ +2 both sides $x - 2 = 12$
$x\quad = 12 + 2$ $\quad\quad\underline{+2\quad +2}$
$x\quad = 14$ $x\quad = 14.$

(**c**) $2x = 9$ ÷2 both sides
$x = 4.5.$

The answer may be negative.
(**d**)$x + 3 = 2$ or $x + 3 = 2$
$x\quad = 2 - 3$ $\quad\quad\underline{-3\quad -3}$
$x\quad = -1$ $x\quad = -1.$

You may need to use fractions
(**e**) $3x = 2$ ÷ 3 both sides
$x = \frac{2}{3}.$

Using a calculator 2 ÷ 3 gives a recurring decimal. $\frac{2}{3}$ is more accurate.

Balancing equations

Keep one side for numbers, the other for variables, and label accordingly.

(**a**) In this example, $n = n$(umbers) b = variable. Tick n or b as you finish each side.

$$\begin{array}{ll} \qquad \mathbf{n} \quad \mathbf{b} & \\ 17 + 2b = 5b + 5 & \text{–2}b \text{ from both sides, tick } n \\ 17 \quad\;\; = 3b + 5 & \text{–5 from both sides, tick } b \\ 12 \quad\;\; = 3b & \div 3 \text{ both sides} \\ 4 \quad\;\;\; = b & \text{Swap around} \\ \quad\;\;\, b = 4. & \end{array}$$

(**b**)
$$\begin{array}{ll} \quad \mathbf{y} \quad \mathbf{n} & \\ \tfrac{1}{4}y = 8 & (\,\tfrac{1}{4}y = y \div 4 \text{ or } \tfrac{y}{4}\,) \\[2mm] \tfrac{y}{4} = 8 & \times 4 \text{ both sides} \\[1mm] \;\; y = 32. & \end{array}$$

(**c**)
$$\begin{array}{ll} -2a = 10 & \div 2 \text{ both sides} \\ -a = 5 & \times -1 \text{ both sides} \\ \;\;\; a = -5. & \end{array}$$

(**d**) It's often easier to keep the variable positive.

$$\begin{array}{ll} 9 = 2x + 1 & \text{–1 both sides} \\ 8 = 2x & \div 2 \text{ both sides} \\ 4 = x & \text{swap round} \\ x = 4. & \end{array}$$

(**e**) Be careful with signs when swapping sides.
$$\begin{array}{l} 6 = -x \\ x = -6. \end{array}$$

(**f**)
$$\begin{array}{ll} x^2 = 25 & \\ x = 5 \textbf{ or } x = -5. & \quad 5 \times 5 = -5 \times -5 = 25 \end{array}$$

Equations viewed vertically

Try this vertical arrangement if you need help with equations. Put headings above columns as before.

(**a**)
$$\begin{array}{rcl}
x & & n \\
2x + 3 & = & 12 \\
-3 & & -3 \\
\hline
2x & = & 9 \\
x & = & 4.5
\end{array}$$
÷ 2 both sides

(**b**)
$$\begin{array}{rcl}
n & & b \\
17 + 2b & = & 5b + 5 \\
-2b & & -2b \\
\hline
17 & = & 3b + 5 \\
-5 & & -5 \\
\hline
12 & = & 3b \\
4 & = & b.
\end{array}$$

or

$$\begin{array}{rcl}
n & & b \\
17 + 2b & = & 5b + 5 \\
-17 & & -17 \\
\hline
2b & = & 5b - 12 \\
-5b & & -5b \\
\hline
-3b & = & -12 \\
b & = & 4.
\end{array}$$

Equations and graphs

Variable	Graph shape
x	straight line
x^2 or x^3	curve

Example graphs

(**a**) $y = x + 1$

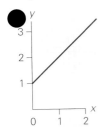

(**b**) $y = 2 - x$

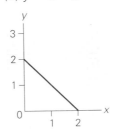

(**c**) $y = x^2$

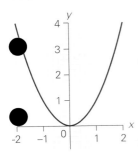

(**d**) $y = x^3$

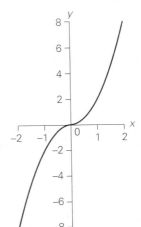

Equations and graphs – continued

(**e**) Draw the graph of the equation $y = 2x + 1$ ($-2 \leqslant x \leqslant 2$). This means that x is any number between -2 and 2. Make a **table of values**, replacing x in the equation by each value in turn.

($-2 \times 2 + 1 = -3, -1 \times 2 + 1 = -1, 0 \times 2 + 1 = 1, 1 \times 2 + 1 = 3, 2 \times 2 + 1 = 5$)

x	-2	-1	0	1	2
y	-3	-1	1	3	5

If x is **N**egative, the line will slope down to the right hand side.

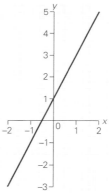

(**f**) Draw the graph of the equation $y = 1 - 2x$ ($-2 \leqslant x \leqslant 2$).

x	**1**	$-2x$	**y**
-2	1	$+4$	5
-1	1	$+2$	3
0	1	$+0$	1
1	1	-2	-1
2	1	-4	-3

Note: tables of values may be set out horizontally or vertically.

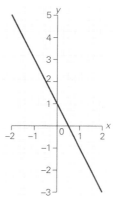

Equally spaced sequences

● **Finding the nth term in equally spaced sequences**

(**a**) (?) 4, 7, 10, 13 ...
Put a ring before the first number, and in it write the number which precedes the first term.

i.e. (1), 4, 7, 10, 13 ...

Then use **DINO** to find the nth term.
DI = Difference = 3, **N** = n (or the letter used in the sequence), **O** = number in ring = 1 and the nth term = $3n + 1$.

(**b**) 2, 8, 14, ... $\rightarrow$ (–4), 2, 8, 14 ...
DI = 6, **N** = n, **O** = –4 and the nth term = $6n – 4$.

Remember, to use DINO the difference between the terms in the first row must be the same.

● **Solving questions involving sequences**

It often helps to find the nth term first.
For example, in the sequence 1, 4, 7, 10, 13 ... find (**a**) the next two terms, (**b**) the nth term, (**c**) the 50th term.

● **Answer** The common difference is 3.
Using DINO DI = 3, N = n, O = –2 so the formula is $3n – 2$.

● (**a**) 16, 19.
(**b**) 3n – 2.
(**c**) 148 (3 × 50 – 2 = 148)

Quadratic sequences

• Two rows of differences mean the sequence involves n^2.
• The second difference divided by two gives the coefficient of n^2.

$$1, \quad 4, \quad 9, \quad 16, \quad 25, \quad 36, \quad \text{Sequence}$$
$$\quad 3, \quad 5, \quad 7, \quad 9, \quad 11, \quad \text{First differences}$$
$$\quad \quad 2, \quad 2, \quad 2, \quad 2, \quad \text{Second differences}$$

Coefficient of $n^2 = 2 \div 2 = 1$, i.e. the nth term $= 1n^2 = n^2$.

Further examples

(**a**) $8, \quad 17, \quad 32, \quad 53, \quad 80, \ldots$
$$\quad 9, \quad 15, \quad 21, \quad 27$$
$$\quad \quad 6, \quad 6, \quad 6$$

Two rows of differences → sequence involves n^2. Coefficient of $n^2 = 6 \div 2 = 3$, i.e. $3n^2 + ?$
Then substitute $n = 1$, $3 \times 1^2 + ? = 8$,
So $? = 5$. Check for $n = 2$. The nth term is $3n^2 + 5$.

(**b**) $2, \quad 6, \quad 12, \quad 20, \quad 30, \quad 42, \quad 56, \ldots$
$$\quad 4, \quad 6, \quad 8, \quad 10, \quad 12, \quad 14,$$
$$\quad \quad 2, \quad 2, \quad 2, \quad 2, \quad 2,$$

Two rows of differences → n^2 sequence, coefficient of $n^2 = 1$.
Substitute $n = 1$, $\quad n^2 + 1 = 2$,
$$n = 2, \quad n^2 + 2 = 6$$
$$n = 3, \quad n^2 + 3 = 12 \text{ etc.}$$
The nth term $= n^2 + n$ or $n(n + 1)$.

Just to recap:

• two rows of differences → sequence involves n^2
• second difference $\div 2 = $ coefficient of n^2
• substitute $n = 1$
• check formula works when $n = 2$, and adjust if necessary.

See also • **Further quadratic sequences** p. 29

Further quadratic sequences

Triangular numbers

$$1, \quad 3, \quad 6, \quad 10, \quad 15, \quad 21, \quad 28 \ldots$$
$$2, \quad 3, \quad 4, \quad 5, \quad 6, \quad 7,$$
$$1, \quad 1, \quad 1, \quad 1, \quad 1,$$

For this sequence the nth term $= \frac{1}{2}n^2 + \frac{1}{2}n$.

This formula is usually written as $\frac{n(n+1)}{2}$.

e.g. $\quad 3^{rd}$ term $= \frac{3 \times 4}{2} = 6$

$\quad\quad 19^{th}$ term $= \frac{19 \times 20}{2} = 190$.

Useful sequences to recognise:

Triangular numbers

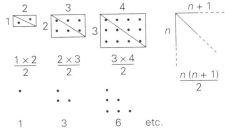

$$\frac{1 \times 2}{2} \quad\quad \frac{2 \times 3}{2} \quad\quad \frac{3 \times 4}{2} \quad\quad \frac{n(n+1)}{2}$$

$$1 \quad\quad\quad 3 \quad\quad\quad\quad 6 \quad\quad \text{etc.}$$

- **Rectangular numbers:** $n(n + 1)$
e.g. 2, 6, 12, 20, ...
- **Fibonacci sequences**:
e.g. 1, 1, 2, 3, 5, 8, 13, ... $\quad 1 + 1 = 2,$
$1 + 2 = 3, 2 + 3 = 5$ etc. (Add the previous two terms to find the next). (You don't need to remember the name!)

See also • Quadratic sequences p. 28

Methods for cracking sequences

Using COSTAS

Cube **O**r **S**quare, **T**imes **A**dd **S**ubtract –
some ideas to try to help spot the pattern!
For example, find the nth term in the
following sequences:

(**a**) 2, 9, 28, 65 ...
(**b**) 2, 16, 54, 128 ...
    Set out the information in a table.

(**a**) 1st 2nd 3rd 4th . . . n^{th}

Try **C**ube (1^3, 2^3 etc.)   1   8   27   64 n^3
                               2   9   28   65

To get from row 1 to row 2, you **A**dd 1 so
the nth term = $n^3 + 1$.

(**b**) 1st 2nd 3rd 4th . . . n^{th}

Try **C**ube (1^3, 2^3 etc.)   1   8   27   64 n^3
                               2   16   54   128

Row 2 is row 1 **T**imes 2 so the
n^{th} term = $2n^3$.

FIBONACCI OTHERS SEQUENCES n^{th} TERM COSTAS QUADRATIC TRIANGULAR NUMBERS

Angles and triangles

Types of triangles

scalene — All three sides and all three angles different

isosceles — Two sides and two angles the same

equilateral — All three sides and all three angles the same

acute angles are < 90°.

obtuse angles are > 90° but < 180°

reflex angles are > 180° but < 360°.

Triangle area

Area of a triangle = ½ base × **perpendicular** height (perpendicuLar means at right angles)

or $\dfrac{\text{base} \times \textbf{perpendicular height}}{2}$.

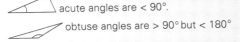

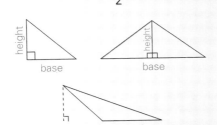

Intersecting and parallel lines

Intersecting lines are lines which cross each other.

FXZ rules

FXZ

Corresponding: you correspond with a riend.

Opposite:

Alternate: know your angles from A to ⟨Z

Straight line: ____x____y____ $x + y = 180°$.

Triangles:  $a + b + c = 180°$.

COAST

Angles of polygons

A **polygon** is any two dimensional straight sided shape, a **regular polygon** is a polygon with all its sides and angles equal.

Interior and exterior angles

The diagram below shows part of a regular polygon (n = number of sides).

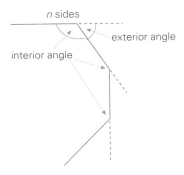

Exterior angle $= \dfrac{360°}{n}$.

Interior angle $= 180°$ − exterior angle.

For example,

Polygon (sides)	Exterior angle	Interior angle
Hexagon (6)	360° ÷ 6 = 60°	180° −60° = 120°
Octagon (8)	360° ÷ 8 = 45°	180° −45° = 135°
Decagon (10)	360° ÷ 10 = 36°	180° −36° = 144°

Circles

Parts of a circle

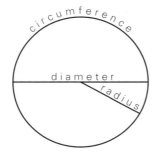

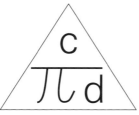

Circumference (c)
Diameter (d)
Radius (r)
$c = \pi d$ or $2\pi r$
$d = \frac{c}{\pi}$.

Look back to page 10 for the cat, table and dog.

Area

$A = \pi r^2$.
"πr squarea gives you the area."

Irregular shapes

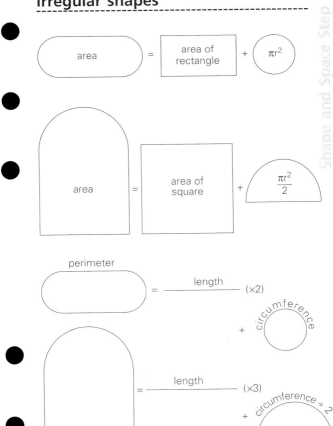

area = area of rectangle + πr^2

area = area of square + $\dfrac{\pi r^2}{2}$

perimeter = length (×2) + circumference

perimeter = length (×3) + circumference ÷ 2

Pythagoras' theorem

Hypotenuse

- The longest side of a right angled triangle.
- Always opposite the right angle.
- To find the **hypotenuse, add** the squares of the other sides, then square root.
- For the **s**horter **s**ides **s**ubtract the squares, then square root.
- "To find the longest side, called the hypot, add the squares of the sides, and square root the lot!"

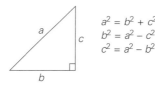

$$a^2 = b^2 + c^2$$
$$b^2 = a^2 - c^2$$
$$c^2 = a^2 - b^2$$

Calculator shows E or Error?

You have probably subtracted a larger number from a smaller, and then tried to square root a negative number. Safety first: always start the calculation with the larger number. In the following examples, find the length marked x.

(**a**)

6.2 cm

$$8.3^2 + 6.2^2 = 107.33$$
$$\sqrt{107.33} = 10.4 \text{ cm}$$

8.3 cm

(**b**)

5.7 cm

x

$$16.9^2 - 5.7^2 = 253.12$$
$$\sqrt{253.12} = 15.9 \text{ cm}$$

16.9 cm

Diagrams not drawn to scale.

See also • **Pythagoras' theorem versus trigonometry** p. 42

Trigonometry basics

● You **must** have a **right angled** triangle.
• **Hypotenuse** (longest side) – always opposite the right angle.
• **Opposite** – side opposite the angle in the question.
● **Adjacent** – remaining side, next to the angle in the question.
• Sine (sin), cosine (cos) and tangent (tan) refer to angles.
● Hypotenuse (hyp), opposite (opp) and adjacent (adj) refer to sides.

• $\sin x = \dfrac{\text{opp}}{\text{hyp}}$, $\cos x = \dfrac{\text{adj}}{\text{hyp}}$, $\tan x = \dfrac{\text{opp}}{\text{adj}}$.

Remember: Some **O**ld **H**ags
Can't **A**lways **H**ide
Their **O**ld **A**ge.
Write this in triplet form, putting the **middle** letter at the top.

Finding angles

● Usually to find an angle, divide, press $=$, then use INV, SHIFT or 2nd F. If your calculator is different, ask your teacher for help.

Trigonometry questions – sides

• Label triangle sides hyp, opp or adj and write out:

as usual.

• Look for the side which the question ignores and cross out the triplets which contain it. The remaining triplet is the one to use.
• Cover or cross out the letter representing the required side or angle then ☒ or ☒ in the usual way.

Remember DO NOT use INV, SHIFT or 2nd F key for finding sides (this is only for angles).

Finding sides

 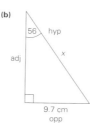

Find x. Diagram not to scale.

Answer

(**a**) O
 T A   Opp = tan 23 × 5.8 = 2.5 cm.

(**b**) O
 S H   Hyp = $\frac{9.7}{\sin 56}$ = 11.7 cm.

Trigonometry questions – angles

Finding angles

Remember

- Opposite, Adjacent and Hypotenuse are sides.
- Sin, Cos and Tan involve angles.
- Label triangle and write:

- Choose triplet as usual and divide to find the sin, cos or tan of the angle.
- Then use the $\boxed{\text{INV}}$, $\boxed{\text{SHIFT}}$ or $\boxed{\text{2}^{\text{nd}}\,\text{F}}$ key.

For example, find the angle x in the diagram below.

Labelling and crossing out as usual gives:

$\cos x = \dfrac{A}{H} = \dfrac{7.5}{10.1} = 0.74257.$

$\boxed{\text{INV}}$ $\boxed{\text{cos}}$ $0.74257 = 42°$.

Calculators aren't all the same – make sure that you can use yours to find angles.

Trigonometry questions – triangles

To use

the triangle must be right angled.

Isosceles triangles

For example, triangle ABC is isosceles.
AB = AC = 9.3 cm, angle ABC = 41°.

(**a**) What is length BC?

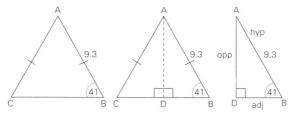

Answer Draw AD perpendicular to BC. Work with half the original triangle.

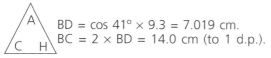

BD = cos 41° × 9.3 = 7.019 cm.
BC = 2 × BD = 14.0 cm (to 1 d.p.).

(**b**) **Find the area of triangle ABC:**

- area = ½BC × AD (or BD × AD)
- use Pythagoras or trigonometry to find AD.

Trigonometry – continued

Using Pythagoras:
$AD^2 = 9.3^2 - 7.02^2 = 37.2096$.
$AD = \sqrt{37.2} = 6.1$ cm.

Using trigonometry:
$AD = \sin 41° \times 9.3 = 6.1$ cm.

Area $= 7.0 \times 6.1 = 42.7$ cm^2.

Recognising questions

Look out for:

- ladders
- flagpoles
- towers
- angles of elevation and depression (see below)
- bearings
- magnitude (i.e. size) of vectors.

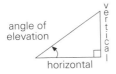

Pythagoras' theorem versus trigonometry

TRIg **N**eeds **A**ngle!
Otherwise, use Pythagoras.

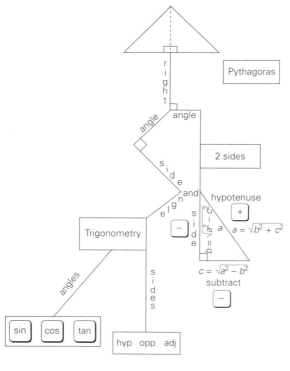

right

angle

angle

Pythagoras

2 sides

side

angle

and

side

hypotenuse

$+$

$a = \sqrt{b^2 + c^2}$

$b = \sqrt{a^2 - c^2}$

a

$c = \sqrt{a^2 - b^2}$

subtract

$-$

$-$

Trigonometry

angles

sides

sin   cos   tan

hyp   opp   adj

Averages and range

Mean: $\dfrac{\text{all values added together}}{\text{total number of values}}$.

Median: middle value when numbers listed from smallest to largest.

Position of median: $\dfrac{\text{number of values}+1}{2}$

Me**d**ian = mi**dd**le   (add one and halve it).

Mode: Most common value.
Range: highest value minus lowest.

For example, for the following set of data:
4, 2, 5, 5, 8, 11, 6, 1, 5, 7, 8, 10:

- the mean = $72 \div 12 = 6$
- the median $\rightarrow$ 1, 2, 4, 5, 5, 5, 6, 7, 8, 8, 10, 11 = 12 values;
  $\dfrac{12+1}{2}$ = 6.5; 6th value = 5, 7th = 6 so the median = 5.5
- the mode = 5
- the range = $11 - 1 = 10$.

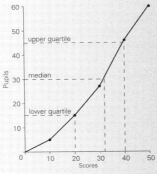

• (For cumulative frequency see over.)

Cumulative frequency

Scores	Frequency	Cumulative frequency
	of pupils	of pupils
$0 < s \le 10$	5	5
$10 < s \le 20$	10	15 (5 + 10)
$20 < s \le 30$	12	27 (15 + 12)
$30 < s \le 40$	19	46 (27 + 19)
$40 < s \le 50$	14	60 (46 + 14)
Total	60	

To plot join the **end points** e.g. at 10, 20, 30 etc. See graph on p.43.

requency on
vertical axis

- **Median:** join line from mid point frequency axis to graph line.
- **Upper quartile:** join line $\frac{3}{4}$ of total frequency to graph line.
- **Lower quartile:** join line $\frac{1}{4}$ of total frequency to graph line.
- **Inter quartile range:** upper quartile – lower quartile.
- **Percentiles:** change values on frequency axis to percentages; using above data the 40th percentile can be read from the graph at $\frac{40}{100} \times 60 = 24$ pupils i.e. a score of 28.

Grouped frequency

Mean of a group frequency

Scores	Frequency (f) (no. of pupils)	Mid interval value (miv) (scores)	f × miv
$0 < s \leqslant 10$	5	5	25
$10 < s \leqslant 20$	10	15	150
$20 < s \leqslant 30$	12	25	300
$30 < s \leqslant 40$	19	35	665
$40 < s \leqslant 50$	14	45	630
Total	60		1770

$0 < s \leqslant 10$ i.e. scores between 1 and 10.
$10 < s \leqslant 20$ i.e. scores between 11 and 20.

Mean = 1770 ÷ 60 = 29.5.

Median group
median position = (60 + 1) ÷ 2 = 30.5.

$1^{st}–5^{th}$ $\quad 6^{th}–15^{th}$ $\quad 16^{th}–27^{th}$ $\quad 28^{th}–46^{th}$ $\quad 47^{th}–60^{th}$
5 $\quad + \quad$ 10 $\quad + \quad$ 12 $\quad + \quad$ 19 $\quad + \quad$ 14 = 60
$\uparrow$ (30.5th value)

median group = $30 < s \leqslant 40$.

Modal group – (i.e. group with most members) = $30 < s \leqslant 40$.

Correlation

Scatter diagrams and line of best fit

- Plot coordinates as given in the question.
- Draw line of best fit so that roughly equal number of points are on each side of the line.

Correlation

- **Strong** if most points are close to the line.
- **Weak** if points are further away.
- **P**ositive correlation slopes u**P**.
- **N**egative correlation slopes dow**N**.
- If **no line** is possible there is **no correlation**.

Strong positive

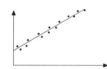

Weak positive

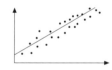

Strong negative

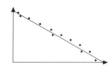

Weak negative

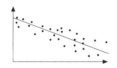

No correlation

Samples and surveys

The **sample** is the group which is being studied.
Think about sample:

- **S**ize (Is it big enough?)
- Is it **R**epresentative? Does it represent all relevant points of view?
- Is it **R**andom? (Do all possible subjects have an equal chance of being chosen?)

Remember these or you'll be **S**o**RR**y.

Surveys

Ask yourself, are the questions:

- **A**mbiguous – i.e. unclear (e.g. "Do you often watch TV?" – "often" is too vague)
- **L**eading – trying to get a certain result ("Don't you agree that…")
- **I**nclusive – all responses must be available? (e.g. "What age are you?" Under 15, 15–20, 25–30 leaves out anyone 21–24 or over 30)
- **B**iased – look at the survey as a whole, is it trying to put across one point of view?
- **1** – each question must only have one answer per respondent (e.g. "Tick your age group." Under 15, 15–20, 20–30, 30 or more – gives two answers for subjects of 20 and 30).

You need these points, for an **ALIB1**!

Fractions and probability

- Calculators vary, but most have $\boxed{a^b/_c}$ keys.
- Practise **before** not during the exam!
- If you have to show your working out check the answer on the calculator.
- Numerator – the number on the top.
- Denominator – number on the bottom.
- Common denominator – same denominator for two or more fractions.

Equivalent fractions

$\frac{1}{2} = \frac{8}{16} = \frac{10}{20} = \frac{25}{50}$ (multiply numerator and denominator by the same number).

Lowest terms

$\frac{12}{15} = \frac{4}{5} \quad \frac{10}{16} = \frac{5}{8}$ (divide numerator and denominator by same number – sometimes called **cancelling**).

Adding/subtracting fractions

All fractions need a common denominator:

$\frac{3}{16} + \frac{1}{8} \rightarrow \frac{3}{16} + \frac{2}{16} = \frac{5}{16}$

$1 - \frac{3}{16} \rightarrow \frac{16}{16} - \frac{3}{16} = \frac{13}{16}$

Multiplying fractions

- Cancel if possible (one number top and bottom each time).
- Multiply numerators and denominators.
- Check again to see if you can cancel.

$\frac{1}{4} \times \frac{2}{5} \rightarrow \frac{1}{2} \times \frac{1}{5} = \frac{1}{10}$.

These techniques are all the fraction techniques you need for probability.

Probability

- Each probability is an **outcome** or **event**.
- Probability of an event =

  $$\frac{\text{no. of times event occurs}}{\text{total number of events}}.$$

- All probabilities must add up to 1.
- Probability of an event **not** happening
  = 1 − probability of the event happening.
- Always use fractions, decimals or percentages (follow the question style).

And ☒ / or ☐

For **independent** (not dependent on each other) events **multiply**. In probability but = and, ("red **but** not striped" ≈ "red **and** not striped").

If outcomes are **mutually exclusive** (not in more than one group at the same time) then **ADD = OR** (Whom do you ad(d)-or(e)?)

For example, a bag contains six red, four green and five blue beads. Eight beads are plastic, the rest are glass. Find the probability of the chosen bead being (a) red, (b) not red, (c) red or blue, (d) pink, (e) glass, (f) why might the probability of the bead being glass and green not be $7/15 \times 4/15$?

Answers

(a) $\frac{6}{15} = \frac{2}{5}$ (b) $1 - \frac{2}{5} = \frac{3}{5}$ (c) $\frac{6}{15} + \frac{5}{15} = \frac{11}{15}$

(Add/or mutually exclusive)

(d) 0   (e) $\frac{7}{15}$

(f) Some might be both glass and green and would be counted twice, (the events are

49

Tree diagrams

The tree diagram below shows the probability of pass/failure in written and practical tests. The probability of passing the written test is 0.4, the probability of passing the practical test is 0.75. The events are independent. Calculate the probability of all possible outcomes.

- Pass written **and** pass practical (i.e. pass both) = 0.4 × 0.75 = 0.3.
- Pass written **and/but** fail practical: 0.4 × 0.25 = 0.1.
- Fail written **but/and** pass practical: 0.6 × 0.75 = 0.45.
- Fail written **and** fail practical (i.e. fail both) = 0.6 × 0.25 = 0.15.
- Check: 0.3 + 0.1 + 0.45 + 0.15 = 1.

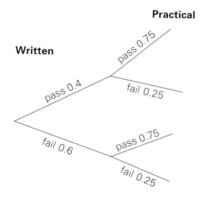

Practical

Written

pass 0.75

pass 0.4

fail 0.25

fail 0.6

pass 0.75

fail 0.25

Imperial and metric units

Length
cm/inches
30 cm ≈ 12 ins or 1 ft

m/inches
1 m ≈ 39 ins

Km ↔ miles
1 km ≈ 5/8 mile
"Journey's end is full of smiles
8 km makes 5 miles."

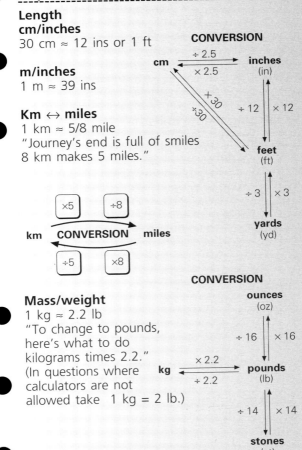

CONVERSION

cm ⟶ inches (in)
÷ 2.5
× 2.5

÷ 12 || × 12

+ 30
+ 30

feet (ft)

÷ 3 || × 3

yards (yd)

km **CONVERSION** miles
×5 ÷8
÷5 ×8

CONVERSION

ounces (oz)

÷ 16 || × 16

Mass/weight
1 kg ≈ 2.2 lb
"To change to pounds,
here's what to do
kilograms times 2.2."
(In questions where
calculators are not
allowed take 1 kg = 2 lb.)

kg ⟶ pounds (lb)
× 2.2
÷ 2.2

÷ 14 || × 14

stones (st)

Imperial and metric units – continued

Capacity/volume
1 l ≈ 1.8 pt
4.5 l ≈ 1 gal

$$\text{litre} \xrightarrow[\times 4.5]{\div 4.5} \text{gal}$$

CONVERSION

Roughly,
"A litre of water is a pint and three quarters".

Changing metric units

Length

÷10	**mm** ↓ ↑	×10	10 mm = 1 cm
÷100	**cm** ↓ ↑	×100	100 cm = 1 m
÷1000	**m** ↓ ↑	×1000	1000 m = 1 km
	km		

> Giving an answer to the nearest 0.1 cm means giving it to the nearest mm.

Weight

÷1000	**g** ↓ ↑	×1000	1000 g = 1 kg
÷1000	**kg** ↓ ↑	×1000	1000 kg = 1 tonne
	tonne		

Capacity/volume

÷1000	**ml** ↓ ↑	×1000	(1 ml = 1 cm³)
	l		1000 ml = 1 l

52

Types of numbers

Factors

Factors are numbers which go (÷) into other numbers exactly. For example, 1, 2, 5 and 10 are factors of 10. (Remember to include ten itself.)

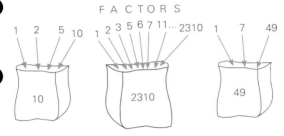

FACTORS

Multiples

Multiples are numbers which factors divide into. Twelve is a multiple of 1, 2, 3, 4, 6, 12. (Remember to include twelve itself.)

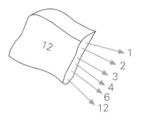

HCF = highest common factor (i.e. biggest number which goes into two or more numbers.)

LCM = lowest common multiple (i.e. smallest number which two or more numbers go into.)

Prime numbers and prime factors

Prime numbers have **exactly two** factors.
For example, numbers 2, 13 and 29.

Note:

• one is not a prime number – its only factor is one itself
• two is the only even prime number
• square numbers >1 have at least 3 factors – themselves, one and their square root so square numbers are never prime numbers.

Prime factors

These are factors which are also prime numbers.

• Two and three are **prime** factors of twelve.
• One, four, six and twelve are factors but **not prime factors** of 12.

Simultaneous equations

Method 1 – graphical

Use a graphical method to solve
$y = 6 - x$,
$y = x + 4$.
Make tables of values and draw the graphs. The solution is their crossing point.
The graphs cross at (1,5) so
$x = 1$, $y = 5$.

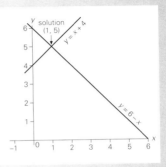

Method 2 – elimination (both variables on same side of equation)

Variable: letter (e.g. x, y).
Coefficient: number (e.g. $3x$, $5y$).

- Choose variable to eliminate and make coefficients the same (multiply if necessary).
- **STOP** (**S**ame **T**ake **O**pposite **P**lus): if the signs are the **S**ame, **T**ake (–) the equations; if the signs are **O**pposite, (one plus, one minus) **P**lus (+) the equations.
- Solve equation to find first variable.
- Replace variable with value to find second variable.
- Use other equation to check both values.

See also • **Equations and graphs** p. 25

Simultaneous equations – continued

Method 2 – elimination (continued)

For example, same sign, same coefficient.

$5x + 2y = 23$ **Equation 1**

$\underline{3x + 2y = 17}$ **Equation 2** (2y in both, same sign)

    $2x = 6$ **1 – 2 S**ame **T**ake

     $x = 3$

Then from **1**

    $5x + 2y = 23$

    $15 + 2y = 23$ ($x = 3$, so $5x = 15$)

       $2y = 8$ ($23 - 15$)

        $y = 4$ ($8 \div 2$)

Check in **2** $(3 \times 3) + (2 \times 4) = 17$.

Same sign, different coefficients.

$5x - 4y = 38$ **Equation 1**

$4x - 2y = 28$ **Equation 2** (×2 **both sides** to

$8x - 4y = 56$ **Equation 3**   make $-4y$)

$8x - 4y = 56$ **3**

$\underline{5x - 4y = 38}$ (**3** – **1**)

$3x = 18$

$x = 6$

Replacing $x = 6$ in **2**

$24 - 2y = 28$

$24 - 28 = 2y$

     $y = -2$

Check in **1** $(5 \times 6) - (4 \times {}^-2)$

$= 30 - {}^-8 = 30 + 8 = 38$.

Method 2 – elimination

Different signs, same coefficients

$10x + 3y = 25$ **Equation 1**
$\underline{4x - 3y = -11}$ **Equation 2** (**1** + **2** **O**pposite **P**lus)
$14x = 14$ $(25 + {}^-11 = 25 - 11 = 14)$
$x = 1$

Replace $x = 1$ in **1**
$10 + 3y = 25$
$3y = 15$
$y = 5$

Check in **2**
$(4 \times 1) - (3 \times 5) = -11.$

Different signs, different coefficients

$5x + 4y = 58$ **Equation 1**
$3x - 5y = 20$ **Equation 2**

Either **1** $\times 3$ and **2** $\times 5 \rightarrow 15x$ in each
or   **1** $\times 5$ and **2** $\times 4 \rightarrow 20y$ in each.

Usually easier to keep positive numbers:
$5x + 4y = 58$ **1** ($\times 5$)
$3x - 5y = 20$ **2** ($\times 4$)

$25x + 20y = 290$ **3**
$\underline{12x - 20y = 80}$ **4** (**O**pposite **P**lus)
$37x = 370$ (**3** + **4**)
$x = 10$

Replace $x = 10$ in **1**

$50 + 4y = 58$
$4y = 8$
$y = 2$

Check in **2** $(3 \times 10) - (5 \times 2) = 20.$

Simultaneous equations – continued

Method 3: Substitution

Use substitution when variables are on different sides of the equation.

(**a**) For example, find x and y.

$$3x + 2y = 48 \qquad \textbf{Equation 1}$$
$$y = x + 4 \qquad \textbf{Equation 2}$$

Replace $2y$ by $2(x + 4)$. **Always put replacement in brackets if it has two or more terms!**

$$3x + 2(x + 4) = 48$$
$$3x + 2x + 8 = 48$$
$$5x + 8 = 48$$
$$5x = 40$$
$$x = 8$$
$$y = 8 + 4 \;\; (y = x + 4 \;\; \textbf{2})$$
$$y = 12$$

(**b**) $\quad 5x + 4y = 22 \quad \textbf{Equation 1}$
$$\qquad\quad 2y = 3x \quad \textbf{Equation 2}$$

(If $2y = 3x$, $4y = 6x$)
$$5x + 6x = 22 \quad \textbf{Substitute} \text{ into } \textbf{1}$$
$$11x = 22$$
$$x = 2$$
$$2y = 3x \quad (\textbf{2}) \;\; 3x = 6$$
$$2y = 6$$
$$y = 3$$

Simultaneous equations – continued

The most common examination questions use elimination so:

Just to recap

- Make coefficients the same for either x or y term ignoring signs (multiply if necessary).
- Use **STOP** (**S**ame **T**ake **O**pposite **P**lus) to find either x or y.
- Replace variable in one equation with this value and solve for second variable.
- Use other equation to **check** both values.

Recognising questions

Questions involving simultaneous equations always involve two different items, for example:

- adults' and children's tickets
- oranges and apples
- large and small coaches.

Simplifying algebra

Simplifying

Simplifying involves putting like with like:

- group like terms together
- remember that signs always cling to their adjoining number.

For example:

- $3x + 4y - 2x \rightarrow 3x - 2x + 4y = x + 4y$
- $12z - 5x + 2z - 3x \rightarrow 12z + 2z - 5x - 3x$
$= 14z - 8x$
- $6a + 3a^2$ cannot be simplified because a and a^2 are different terms.

Multiplying out (or expanding) brackets

Single brackets: basics (usually 2 terms)

- $3(2x + 4) = 3 \times 2x + 3 \times 4 = 6x + 12$
- $4(3m - g) = 4 \times 3m - 4 \times g = 12m - 4g$
- $c(3c + 4) = c \times 3c + c \times 4 = 3c^2 + 4c$
- $-2(a + 8) = -2 \times a + -2 \times 8 = -2a - 16$
- $2(x - 3) + 11 = 2x - 6 + 11 = 2x + 5.$

A bracket without a number in front? Put a **1**.

$7 - (3x + 2) = 7 - 1(3x + 2) = 7 - 3x - 2$

Note: Take care with signs: $-1 \times 2 = -2$.
$7 - 3x - 2 = 7 - 2 - 3x = 5 - 3x.$
$13y - (5y - 6) = 13y - 1(5y - 6)$
$13y - 5y + 6 = 8y + 6.$ $(^-1 \times ^-6 = 6)$

- **Algebra basics** p. 21
- **Balancing equations** p. 23

Expanding and simplifying expressions

Double brackets (usually 3 terms)

x^2, x and a number without x.

Example (**a**) $(b + 5)(b + 3)$

First **O**ut **I**n **L**ast (**FOIL**)
$b \times b + b \times 3 + 5 \times b + 5 \times 3$
$$= b^2 + 3b + 5b + 15$$
$$= b^2 + 8b + 15.$$

Example (**b**) $(a + 2)(a - 3)$

(**F**)   (**O**)   (**I**)   (**L**)
$a \times a + a \times -3 + 2 \times a + 2 \times -3$
$= a^2 - 3a \quad + 2a \quad\quad - 6$
$= a^2 - a - 6.$

Example (**c**) $(z - 2)(z - 5)$
$$= z^2 - 5z - 2z + 10$$
$$= z^2 - 7z + 10. \quad (^-2 \times ^-5 = 10)$$

Using a grid

$\times$	b	$+5$
b	b^2	$+5b$
$+3$	$+3b$	$+15$

$(b + 5)(b + 3)$
$= b^2 + 3b + 5b + 15$
$= b^2 + 8b + 15.$

$\times$	a	$+2$
a	a^2	$+2a$
-3	$-3a$	-6

$(a + 2)(a - 3)$
$= a^2 - 3a + 2a - 6$
$= a^2 - a - 6.$

$\times$	z	-2
z	z^2	$-2z$
-5	$-5z$	$+10$

$(z - 2)(z - 5)$
$= z^2 - 5z - 2z + 10$
$= z^2 - 7z + 10$
$(^-2 \times ^-5 = 10)$

How to factorise

Questions usually say:
  factorise / factorise fully.

Factorising expressions

Example (**a**) $3gh + 6gk$

- Three is a common factor.
- Write three outside the brackets: $3(gh + 2gk)$.
- Letter g is a common factor.
- Write g beside the three: $3g(h + 2k)$.
- There are no more common factors, so $3gh + 6gk = 3g(h + 2k)$.
- Multiply out to check [$3g(h + 2k) = 3gh + 6gk$].

Example (**b**) $8a^2 - 2ax$
$2(4a^2 - ax) \rightarrow 2a(4a - x)$ $(a^2 - ax = aa - ax)$.
So $8a^2 - 2ax = 2a(4a - x)$ (then multiply and check).

Example (**c**) $10x^2y - 15xy^2 \rightarrow 5(2x^2y - 3xy^2) \rightarrow 5x(2xy - 3y^2) \rightarrow 5xy(2x - 3y)$.
So $10x^2 - 15xy^2 = 5xy(2x - 3y)$ (then multiply and check).
Write "1" inside the brackets if all factors of a term are outside.

Example (**d**)
$6y^2z - 2y \rightarrow 2(3y^2z - y) \rightarrow 2y(3yz - 1)$. So $6y^2z - 2y = 2y(3yz - 1)$ (then multiply to check).

Gradients

Gradients show the **rate of change**, i.e. vertical units **per** horizontal unit. Examples include:

- exchange rate in dollars **per** pound (a)
- speed in km **per** hour (b).

(a)

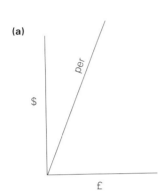

(b)

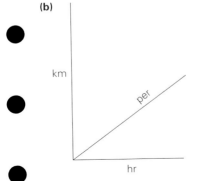

Equation of a line

Equations of a line are often written as **y = mx + c**, where **m** stands for the **gradient** and **c** stands for the **constant** which is the value at the y intercept.

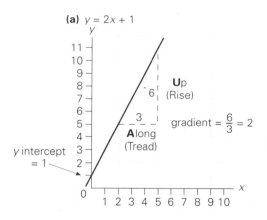

(a) $y = 2x + 1$

Up (Rise)

Along (Tread)

gradient $= \frac{6}{3} = 2$

y intercept = 1

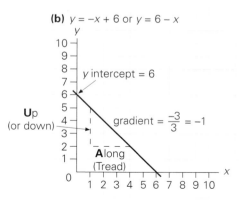

(b) $y = -x + 6$ or $y = 6 - x$

y intercept = 6

Up (or down)

Along (Tread)

gradient $= \frac{-3}{3} = -1$

GRADients are **U**p over **Al**ong – **GRADUAL** or Gradients are **GROT**ty – **G**radients are **R**ise **O**ver **T**read.

Quadrilaterals

	Shape	Lines of symmetry Reflections	Order of symmetry Rotations
Square	area = l × w, l, w	4	4
Rectangle	area = l × w, l, w	2	2
Parallelogram	area = b × h, height, base	0	2

Quadrilaterals – continued

Shape	Lines of symmetry Reflections	Order of symmetry Rotations
Kite	1	1
Rhombus	2	2
Trapezium	0 or 1	1 1

Area of a trapezium
$= \dfrac{(a + b)}{2} \times \text{height}$

Volume

Prisms

A **prism** is a 3D shape which cuts into identical slices, i.e. **cross sections**.

Volume of a prism = area of cross section × length

Prism

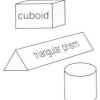

Cross section

 or

Volume

V = **V**olume (or capacity).
A = **A**rea (of cross section).
T = **T**he other one, i.e. the linear dimension (usually length, but could be width, height, depth or thickness).

Nets

Three dimensional shapes opened flat, not including flaps, **note** some shapes have lids – e.g. unopened cylinders.

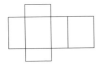

Cuboid

Triangular prism

Cylinder with two ends

Some don't – e.g. fish tanks and most bins. When drawing nets there is often more than one right answer.

Volume – continued

Example (**a**) A cylinder has a radius of 75 cm and a height of 85 cm. Find its volume in litres to the nearest litre.

Volume = area × height.
A = area of circle.
The other one = height.
$\pi r^2 \times h = \pi \times 75^2 \times 85 =$
1 502 074 cm^3
1000 cm^3 = 1 litre so
1 502 074 ÷ 1000 = 1502 l to the nearest litre.

Example (**b**) A cuboid with base 25 cm × 30 cm contains 8.5 litres of water. How deep is the water?

Volume = 8.5 l = 8500 cm^3
Area = 25 cm × 30 cm = 750 cm^2
The other one = depth
Depth = 8500 cm^3 ÷ 750 cm^2 =
11.3 cm (to 1 d.p.).

Example (**c**) A cylinder height 25 cm contains 5.2 litres of liquid. Find its radius.

Firstly, find the area of the cross section.

Area = **V**olume ÷ **T**he other one
i.e. height.
A = 5200 cm^3 ÷ 25 = 208 cm^2

Now $A = \pi r^2$ so $\dfrac{A}{\pi} = r^2$ $r = \sqrt{\dfrac{A}{\pi}}$

$r = \sqrt{\dfrac{208}{\pi}} = \sqrt{66.2}$ so $r = 8.1$ cm (1 d.p.).

Bearings

- Start by facing north.
- Turn clockwise.
- Always use three digits to measure bearings.

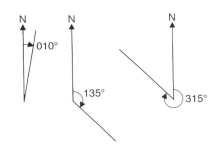

Example (**a**) The bearing of T from P is 063°.
Find the bearing of P from T.
Draw sketch as follows:

- start **from** P and draw a north facing line
- sketch angle as shown and mark T
- draw N line from T parallel to PN.

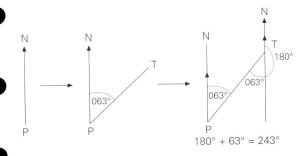

180° + 63° = 243°

The bearing of P **from** T = 180° + 63° = 243°.

Loci

The **locus** of a point is the path that it makes.

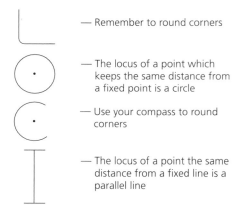

— Remember to round corners

— The locus of a point which keeps the same distance from a fixed point is a circle

— Use your compass to round corners

— The locus of a point the same distance from a fixed line is a parallel line

Overlapping regions

In the diagram below PQRS represents a bedroom. The table must be at least 2 m from the wall PQ and less than 4 m from a lamp at P. Shade the region where the table could be.

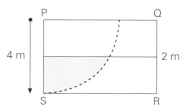

In diagrams, boundaries are solid lines, dotted lines are used for arcs. Questions often say ... at least/more than ... **or** less than ... 2m.

Loci and constructions

A **perpendicular bisector** cuts a line in half at right angles (bisect = cut in half, perpendicu**L**ar = at right angles).

Example loci question
ABCD is a rectangle, shade the region which is nearer AD than BC.

 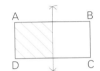

Bisecting angles

60° angles

30° angle Draw an angle of 60° – then bisect.

Example loci question
Shade the region which is nearer FJ than it is to HJ.

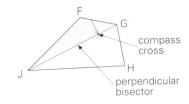

compass cross

perpendicular bisector

Shapes and transformations

Congruent shapes are identical, i.e. the same shape and size.

Similar shapes – one shape is an enlargement of the other. To find its scale factor:

- Choose corresponding sides.
- Then **S**econd (i.e. new) **O**ver **F**irs**T** (i.e. old).
- You are **SOFT** in the head if you forget!

There are four transformations which you need for GCSE:

- reflection
- rotation
- enlargement
- translation.

An object which has been **transformed** is called its **image** or **mapping**.

If you have a diagram with point p the question might say:

- give the image of p under the transformation ...
- what point does p map to under the transformation ...
- what transformation maps p on to p'?

Reflections

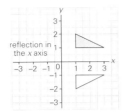

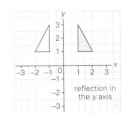

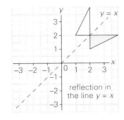

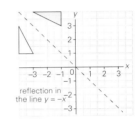

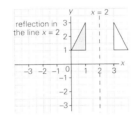

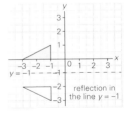

State the mirror line e.g. x axis, $y = -x$, $x = 4$ etc.

Rotations

You can use tracing paper to help you find
the centre of a rotation.
State:

- the centre of rotation
- the angle of rotation
- the direction, clockwise or anti clockwise
(unless 180°).

Examples

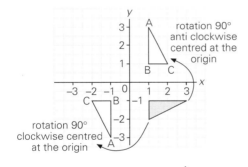

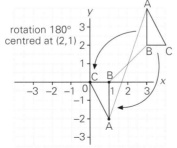

Enlargements

Questions involving similar shapes refer to **enlargements**. To find the centre of enlargement join the points of the object to those of its image.

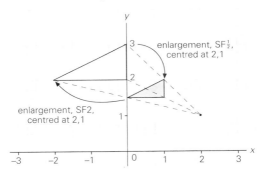

Note if the scale factor (SF) is <1 the image is smaller, but it's still called an enlargement!

Example ABC and DEF are similar. (**a**) Find EF to 1 d.p. (**b**) If angle ACB = 25° what is angle DFE?

Answer (**a**) Scale factor: = 1.6

$$\frac{DE}{AB} = \frac{6.9}{4.3} = 1.6 \rightarrow EF = 5.8 \times 1.6 = 9.3 \text{ cm.}$$

(**b**) Angle DFE = angle ACB = 25°.

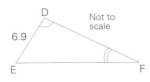

75

Translations

A translation moves a shape from one place to
another without changing its size or direction.
When using a translation vector go **across**
first – **VC**, you measure **V**ectors like
Coordinates.

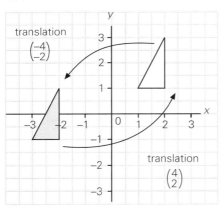

How to transform your marks!

One mark for correct identification	Extra marks for identification		Total
reflection	+1	reflection line (e.g. x. axis, y = x etc).	2
rotation	+3	centre, direction, angle of rotation.	4
enlargement	+2	centre and scale factor of enlargement.	3
translation	+1	vector for translation.	2

Frequency diagrams

Pie charts

- All angles usually total 360°.
- All percentages usually total 100%.
- You may need to round up or down, so totals may not be exact.

How to solve pie chart questions:

X-Direct is quick and easy! For example, 480 people took part in a survey.

(**a**) How many people would 30° represent?
(**b**) What angle would represent 60 people?
(**c**) What percentage of the sample do 126° represent?

Answers

(**a**) People	Degrees	(**b**) People	Degrees
480	360	480	360
$\dfrac{480 \times 30}{360}$	30		$\dfrac{360 \times 60}{480}$
= 40 people		60	= 45°

(**c**)
Degrees	%
360	100
126	$\dfrac{100 \times 126}{360}$
	= 35%

See also • **X-Direct method** p. 11

Frequency charts

Histograms

Scores	Frequency
0 < s ≤ 10	5
10 < s ≤ 20	10
20 < s ≤ 30	12
30 < s ≤ 40	19
40 < s ≤ 50	14

At intermediate level histograms look the same as bar charts.

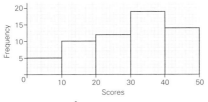

Frequency polygons

Here is the same data presented as a frequency polygon.

- Imagine a bar chart.
- Mark mid point of top of each imaginary bar and join the points with a straight line.
- Ask your teacher when to join the line to the axis.

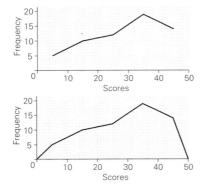

Fractions

Top heavy fractions

$\frac{35}{8}$, $\frac{13}{6}$ numerator > denominator.

Mixed numbers

$4\frac{3}{8}$, $2\frac{1}{6}$ a whole number and a fraction.

Converting top heavy fractions into mixed numbers and vice versa.

$\frac{35}{8} = 35 \div 8 = 4\ r\ 3 = 4\frac{3}{8}.$ $4\frac{3}{8} = \frac{4 \times 8 + 3}{8} = \frac{35}{8}.$

$\frac{13}{6} = 2\ r\ 1 = 2\frac{1}{6}.$ $2\frac{1}{6} = \frac{2 \times 6 + 1}{6} = \frac{13}{6}.$

Adding/subtracting fractions

- All fractions need a common denominator.
- Add/subtract the whole numbers and the fractions where possible.
- Change whole numbers to fractions if necessary when subtracting.
- Change top heavy fractions to mixed numbers and cancel if necessary.

$5\frac{3}{16} + 2\frac{7}{8} \rightarrow 7\frac{3}{16} + \frac{14}{16} \rightarrow 7\frac{17}{16} = 8\frac{1}{16}.$

$7\frac{1}{5} - 2\frac{3}{4} \rightarrow 5\frac{1}{5} - \frac{3}{4} \rightarrow 5\frac{4}{20} - \frac{15}{20} \rightarrow 4\frac{24}{20} - \frac{15}{20} = 4\frac{9}{20}.$

Fractions and product of prime factors

Multiplying/dividing fractions

- Change any mixed numbers to top heavy fractions.
- If dividing turn the second fraction upside down. (**d** in second not first.)
- Cancel if possible (one number top and bottom each time).
- Multiply numerators and denominators.
- Change back to mixed numbers and cancel if possible.

$$2\frac{1}{4} \times 2\frac{2}{5} \rightarrow \frac{9}{4} \times \frac{12}{5} \rightarrow \frac{9}{1} \times \frac{3}{5} \rightarrow \frac{27}{5} = 5\frac{2}{5}$$

$$6\frac{1}{4} \div 1\frac{2}{3} \rightarrow \frac{25}{4} \div \frac{5}{3} \rightarrow \frac{25}{4} \times \frac{3}{5} \rightarrow \frac{5}{4} \times \frac{3}{1} \rightarrow \frac{15}{4} = 3\frac{3}{4}.$$

Product of prime factors

For example, write 180 as a product of prime factors.

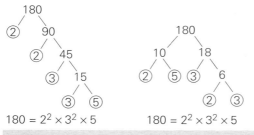

$$180 = 2^2 \times 3^2 \times 5 \qquad 180 = 2^2 \times 3^2 \times 5$$

- Split each number into pairs of factors.
- Ring the prime numbers.
- Split each number until every strand ends in a prime number.
- Write each number in power form.
- There is often more than one route.

See also • Prime numbers and prime factors p.54

Rearranging formulae

Basics

- Formulae behave like other equations.
- Circle the subject and its sign.
- Leave where it is unless it's negative or on the bottom.
- Move any other letters or numbers one term at a time to the other side of the equation.
- **Remember: change sides, change sign.**
- **Plus $\leftrightarrow$ minus, multiply $\leftrightarrow$ divide.**

For example, make x the subject in all equations on pages 81–82.

Plus $\leftrightarrow$ minus

- $c = b + x \rightarrow c - b = x \rightarrow x = c - b.$
- $d = x - a \rightarrow d + a = x \rightarrow x = d + a.$
- $f = a - x \rightarrow f + x = a \rightarrow x = a - f.$

(start by making x positive).

Multiply $\leftrightarrow$ divide

- $a = dx \rightarrow \frac{a}{d} = x \rightarrow x = \frac{a}{d}.$

- $b = \frac{x}{g} \rightarrow bg = x \rightarrow x = bg.$

- $f = \frac{y}{x} \rightarrow fx = y \rightarrow x = \frac{y}{f}.$

(start by getting x to the top for a short cut: swap $f = \frac{y}{x}$ to $x = \frac{y}{f}$).

Squares/square roots

- $x^2 = c \rightarrow x = \pm\sqrt{c}.$

- $x^2 + d = t \rightarrow x^2 = t - d \rightarrow x = \pm\sqrt{t-d}.$

See also • **Equation basics** p.22

Rearranging formulae – continued

Note

Square or square root everything on that side of the equation.

- $\sqrt{x} = f \rightarrow x = f^2$.

- $\sqrt{x} = s - w \rightarrow x = (s - w)^2$.

Note remember the brackets.

- $ax^2 = v \rightarrow x^2 = \dfrac{v}{a} \rightarrow x = \sqrt{\dfrac{v}{a}}$.

  Note $\sqrt{\text{the whole term}}$.

Plus ↔ minus   multiply ↔ divide

- $a = cx - d \rightarrow a + d = cx \rightarrow$
  $\frac{a+d}{c} = x \rightarrow x = \frac{a+d}{c}$.

- $h = kx + b \rightarrow h - b = kx \rightarrow$
  $\frac{h-b}{k} = x \rightarrow x = \frac{h-b}{k}$.

- $m = j - xy \rightarrow m + xy = j \rightarrow$
  $xy = j - m \rightarrow x = \frac{j-m}{y}$.

FaBuLouS formulae

- **F**ractions – get rid of by multiplying.
- **B**rackets – multiply out.
- **L**ike terms – get what you want on one side, everything else to other.
- **S**ort it out – probably **S**quaring or **S**quare rooting.

How to factorise double brackets

For factorising quadratic expressions i.e.
$x^2 + bx + c$ $\qquad x^2 + bx - c$
$x^2 - bx + c$ $\qquad x^2 - bx - c$
find 2 numbers which **multiply** $\to c$ (the constant) and **add/subtract** $\to b$ (coefficient of x).

Look at the sign of the constant

- $+c \to$ both brackets have same sign
(plus = same: both four letters)
- $-c \to$ each pair of brackets have different sign (minus = different).

A positive constant means that both brackets have the same sign. The sign of the brackets is the **same** as that of the x **coefficient**.

Example (**a**) Factorise $x^2 + 8x + 12$

- Constant +12 so both brackets same sign.
- Coefficient +8 so both brackets +.
- Split constant into pairs of factors.
- Factors of 12 are 1, 2, 3, 4, 6, 12.
- Two numbers need to multiply $\to 12$:
$6 \times 2 = 12$.
- Two numbers need to **add/subtract** $\to 8$:
$6 + 2 = 8$.

How to factorise double brackets –
continued

$$+8$$

x^2	$+12$
x	$+6$
x	$+2$

Result = $(x + 6)(x + 2)$.

Example (**b**) Factorise $x^2 - 8x + 12$

- $+12$ is constant so both brackets same sign.
- -8 coefficient so both brackets $-$.
- Factors of 12 are 1, 2, 3, 4, 6, 12.
- Two numbers need to **multiply** $\rightarrow 12$:
$-6 \times -2 = 12$.
- Two numbers need to **add/subtract** $\rightarrow$
-8: $-6 - 2 = -8$.

$$-8$$

x^2	$+12$
x	-6
x	-2

Result = $(x - 6)(x - 2)$.

Solving by factorising

Make sure you can factorise (see references).

$x^2 + 3x - 10 = 0$

$(x + 5)(x - 2) = 0$

$x + 5 = 0$ **or** $x - 2 = 0$

$x = -5$ **or** $x = 2$.

Rearrange if necessary so that the equation is in the form $x^2 \pm bx \pm c = 0$

First check:

- equation = 0
- x^2 is positive.

Making equation = 0

$x^2 - 8x = 20$

$x^2 - 8x - 20 = 0$

$(x - 10)(x + 2) = 0$

$x = 10 \quad x = -2$.

Making x^2 positive

$x = 6 - x^2$

$0 = 6 - x^2 - x$

$x^2 + x - 6 = 0$

$(x + 3)(x - 2) = 0$

$x = -3 \quad x = 2$.

Just to recap

- Make sure that equation = 0 and x^2 is positive.
- Factorise.
- Make sure each term in turn = 0, and solve.

See also • **How to factorise** p. 62
• **How to factorise double brackets** pp. 83–84

Quadratic equations

We have used x and x^2 but the rules apply to any variable.

Quadratic equations have two values for x

For example
(**a**) $(x + 5)\,(x - 2) = 0$

If two numbers multiplied together $= 0$, one of them must be 0.
$(x + 5) \times (x - 2) = 0$ so $x + 5 = 0$ **or** $x - 2 = 0$.
$x = -5$ **or** $x = 2$.

(**b**) $x(x - 4) = 0$
$x = 0$ **or** $x - 4 = 0$
$x = 0$ **or** $x = 4$.

(**c**) $(2x + 5)\,(x + 3) = 0$
$2x + 5 = 0$ **or** $x + 3 = 0$
$2x = -5$ **or** $x = -3$
$x = -2.5$ **or** $x = -3$.

Quadratic graphs

For example, draw the graph of
$y = x^2 - 3x$ $(-1 \leq x \leq 4)$ and find:

- (a) x when $y = 3$
- (b) the minimum value of x
- (c) the values of x for which $y \leq 0$.

Answers Make a table of values for x
between -2 and 4.

x	-1	0	1	2	3	4
x^2	1	0	1	4	9	16
$-3x$	3	0	-3	-6	-9	-12
y	4	0	-2	-2	0	4

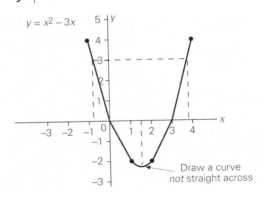

$y = x^2 - 3x$

Draw a curve *not* straight across

Answers

- (a) $x = -0.8$ and 3.8 approximately
- (b) $x = 1.5$
- (c) x is between 0 and 3.

Mind Maps – algebra/graphs

Equations – algebra

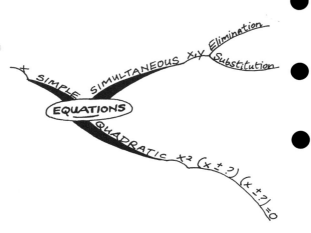

Equations – graphs

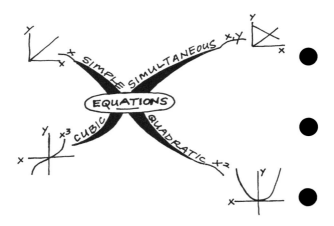

Inequalities

$-3 \leq x \leq 2$: x is $B \leq TW \leq \leq N$ -3 and 2.

$-2 < x \leq 4$: x is $B < TW \leq \leq N$ -2 and 4, but excluding -2 itself.

Inequalities and algebra

They often work like equations.

$x + 3 < 7$ $x - 8 \geq 20$
   $\downarrow$ -3 both sides $\downarrow$ $+8$ both sides
$x < 4$ x ≥ 28.

BUT if you swap both sides, the inequality reverses.

A horse > a mouse so a mouse < a horse.
$3 > x$ so $x < 3$.

Note: if you × or ÷ by a negative number the inequality sign reverses.

$-6 < 2$ so $6 > -2$ (× both sides by -1)

Be careful with square numbers

For example, find values of x so that
(**a**) $x^2 \leq 25$ (**b**) $x^2 \geq 25$.

Answer (a)

$-5 \leq x \leq 5$
x is $B \leq TW \leq \leq N$ -5 and 5

(**b**)

$x \leq -5$, $x \geq 5$
x is $\leq \geq TSI \geq E$ -5 and 5

Inequalities and regions

When y is positive on the left side of the inequality graph and ABOVE the equation line, $y > x + 2$.
When y is BELOW the line $y < x + 2$.

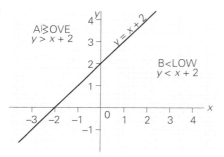

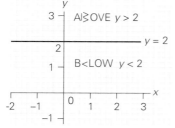

Note
x value changes but y is always $= 2$.

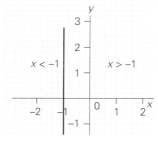

Note
y value changes but x is always $= -1$.

Shape and Space   Step 3

Dimensions
Imagine all units are cm, cm^2 or cm^3:
± within but not across dimensions:

- **the answer stays in the same dimension**
- cm + cm = cm (e.g. 3 cm + 4 cm = 7 cm)
- cm − cm = cm (or zero)
- cm + cm^2 = nonsense (10 cm + 2 cm^2 = ?)
- similarly cm^2 + cm^3 = ? (12 cm^2 + 3 cm^3 = ?)
- length + length = length
- area + area = area
- volume + volume = volume.

×/÷ within and across dimensions:

- **the answer is in a different dimension**
- cm × cm = cm^2 (length × length = area)
- cm^3 ÷ cm^2 = cm (volume ÷ area = length)
- length × length = area
- area ÷ length = length
- length × area = volume
- volume ÷ length = area
- volume ÷ area = length.

Multiplying or dividing by fractions, π and whole numbers do not change the number of dimensions, merely the size.

For example, $\frac{3}{4}$ cm, 10 cm or π cm are all measures of length.

Only by removing the whole numbers, fractions and π and by changing the remaining letters to cm, cm^2 or cm^3 would a change in dimension be achieved.

Dimensions – continued

Examples

Letters a, b and c represent lengths. State, with a reason whether the following are formulae for length, area or volume or none of these.

Hint: single letter $\rightarrow$ cm; two letters or letter^2 $\rightarrow$ cm^2; three letters or letter^3 $\rightarrow$ cm^3.
e.g. a, b, or c $\rightarrow$ cm; ab, c^2 etc. $\rightarrow$ cm^2; aab, abc, ac^2, b^3 $\rightarrow$ cm^3.

- $3a + \pi c \rightarrow a + c \rightarrow$ cm + cm
= length + length = length.
- $10a^2 + 5ac \rightarrow a^2 + ac \rightarrow$ cm^2 + cm $\times$ cm
$\rightarrow$ cm^2 + cm^2 = area + area = area.
- $0.5a(c + b) \rightarrow$ cm (cm + cm)
= length (length + length) = length (length)
or length $\times$ length = area.
- $\pi ac + 3b^2c \rightarrow ac + b^2c \rightarrow ac + bbc$
$\rightarrow$ cm^2 + cm^3 = area + volume (impossible).
- $\pi ab \times \frac{1}{2}bc \rightarrow$ cm^2 $\times$ cm^2 = cm^4 = area $\times$
area = 4 dimensions therefore not length, area or volume.

Dimensions and indices

Remember cm = cm^1 and use **TIP** and **DIM** (see reference).

- cm^2 $\times$ cm^1 = cm^3 (area $\times$ length
= volume).
- cm^3 $\div$ cm^1 = cm^2 (volume $\div$ length
= area).
- cm^3 + cm^2 cannot be simplified in index form, volume + area = nonsense.

Plan and elevation

Imagine a solid glass object as shown in the figure.

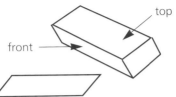

Now draw dotted lines to represent any lines which you would see looking down through it. This is a **plan,** i.e. an object viewed from the top and flattened.

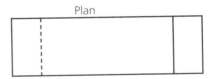

Plan

Elevation

Elevation – an object viewed face on from the front – **front elevation**.

When the object is viewed from the side – **side elevation**.

Tessellation

Shapes **tessellate** when they fit together around a point without a gap. They may be the same shape, e.g. hexagons or they may be a mixture, e.g. octagons and squares.

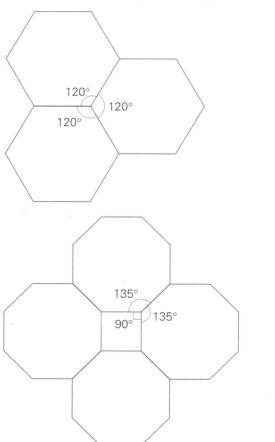

Nearly there now!

Quick quiz

1 How many Maths exams will you have?
(Ans. Two/three/four)

2 Have you done Maths course work?
(Ans. Yes/No)

3 If you answered "yes", was it good
enough for your hoped for grade?
(Ans. Yes/No)

(If "no", ask your teacher what you can do
about it.)

4 Do you have a maths aural exam?
(Ans. Yes/No)

5 Do you have a non-calculator paper?
(Ans. Yes/No)

(If "yes", to (4) and/or (5), brush up on
those times tables.)

6 Can you do   (a) trial and improvement,
using a calculator?
(b) long multiplication?
(c) long division?

(If "no" to any, try to fit them in now.)

7 Do you know the dates of your exams?
(Ans. Yes/No)

8 Do you know what time each of them will
start? (Ans. Yes/No)

(Make sure in good time that you can
answer "Yes" to 7 and 8.)

You've made it!

Well done! You've finished the syllabus.
Now keep in practice by doing as many past papers as you can.

And finally ... be prepared! ...
The day before the exam check that:

- your batteries work if your calculator isn't solar powered
- your ruler hasn't developed a crack or chip
- you have at least one pencil with a lethally sharp point and
- a sharpener for emergency use!
- your pen hasn't sprung a leak and
- you have a spare just in case!
- your compasses don't wobble, or you can beg, borrow or steal ones that don't
- you can find your protractor or angle measurer – have you tried looking under the bed ... behind the fridge ... inside the dog?

... and really finally finally ...

Good luck! Though if you've got this far, you probably won't need it.